Dedication

To my Dad, John Biondo, who instilled in me his passion for life, old cars, and the wonders of "the road."

&

To a man with a giant appetite who turned out to be one of the most entertaining storytellers I've ever known, my dad, Albert Eng.

About the Authors

John Eng was bitten by the *film bug* while still in high school. When a friend of his brother appeared with an 8mm movie camera, they were off making kung-fu movies on the rooftops of New York. While attending the School of Visual Arts, he answered an ad by a Hungarian puppet animator looking for a model builder. This began John's professional life with film, special effects, and animation.

John relocated to Los Angeles in 1981 where he produced, production designed, and supervised special effects on a number of independent feature films before he was offered a steady design position on the sci-fi series, *The Max Headroom Show*. He then directed the animated underground comedy *Duckman* before producing *The Real Adventures of Jonny Quest* at Hanna-Barbera. At Nickelodeon, John created three pilots, then directed *Globehunters,* a direct-to-DVD feature. In 2001, he co-directed the third Rugrats feature, *Rugrats Go Wild*.

Paralleling this, John shared his love for travel, local history, and photography with Adriene Biondo by driving to every corner of California and beyond. Before digital, John used large format cameras in addition to modified antique postcard cameras to shoot 6 x 14 cm panoramic images. John's photography has appeared in L.A. Magazine, Dwell, and CA Modern magazine.

For Adriene Biondo, there's never been anything cozier than sharing a hot cup o' joe. Even cozier if it's in a mom and pop coffee shop off an abandoned highway warmed by an old flickering neon sign. Luckily, she grew up in 1960s and 1970s Los Angeles. Back then, amazing coffee shops and drive-ins were everywhere! Her family spent many happy weekends traveling in "Ol' Yeller," their trusty 1952 Ford station wagon. As these places began to disappear, Adriene realized she was witnessing the end of an era, both culturally and architecturally. Eventually she found her way into historic preservation and began working with the Los Angeles Conservancy, the nation's largest non-profit historic preservation organization. An award-winning preservationist, Adriene has directed significant projects that have been honored by the State Office of Historic Preservation and California Preservation Foundation. In 2008, she accepted the President's Award for leading the effort to rebuild the landmark 1958 Harvey's Broiler. By day, she's a freelance photographer and public relations liaison for CA Modern, an architectural/lifestyle magazine based in San Francisco. By night, you might catch her playing cocktail piano in one of the restaurants featured in this book.

Southern California Eats

John Eng

Adriene Biondo

Schiffer Publishing Ltd

4880 Lower Valley Road Atglen, PA 19310

Acknowledgments

A book requires the help and contribution from so many individuals and organizations that any attempt to list them all is sure to fail. So here we go. Sincere thanks to all the coffee shop, restaurant owners, and support staff for their generous help, especially Joe Becker, Jay Falconer, Roy Hall, Jane Hendricks, Eva Lopez, Jim Louder, Biff Naylor, Minnie Ortner, Manny Romero, Alicia and Arturo Sanchez, Lonzia Shay, Yvonne of J's, and Charlie of Ludlow.

Our warmest thanks to Stan Abrams, Ron Binkley, John Biondo Sr., Eldon and Luanna Davis, Helen Fong, Alan Hess, Tony Hortenstein, Jack and Jan Laxer, Jim McSwan, Buddy Worth, the Los Angeles Conservancy for their appreciation of our architectural treasures, our friends at the Modern Committee for their relentless passion in the preservation of modern architecture, along with the Friends of Johnie's and Coalition to Rebuild the Broiler, Roadside Peek, and all the nice folks at the San Fernando Valley Historical Society.

And finally, we thank our editor, Tina Skinner, and publisher Peter B. Schiffer for believing in us and accepting our oddball idea for this book.

Disclaimer

The text and products pictured in this book are from the collection of the author of this book, its publisher, or various private collectors. This book is not sponsored, endorsed, or otherwise affiliated with any of the companies whose products are represented herein. They include (AMF, Bob's Big Boy, Chris' & Pitt's, Clearman's Restaurants, Clifton's, Dinah's, Du-par's, Encounter/Los Angeles International Airport, Kona, Madonna Inn, Musso & Frank's, 94th Aero Squadron, Norms, Original Pancake House, Pann's, Philippe's, Ship's, Smokehouse, Tony's on the Pier, Trader Vic's, Vince's Spaghetti, Warehouse, among others). This book is derived from the authors' independent research.

Cover image: Bun 'n Burger, Alhambra, 1940, Walter Zick, architect. *Photo: John Eng.*

Designed by John Eng
Layout by John P. Cheek
Type set in Gill Sans MT

ISBN: 978-0-7643-3332-3
Printed in China

Schiffer Books are available at special discounts for bulk purchases for sales promotions or premiums. Special editions, including personalized covers, corporate imprints, and excerpts can be created in large quantities for special needs. For more information contact the publisher:

Published by Schiffer Publishing Ltd.
4880 Lower Valley Road
Atglen, PA 19310
Phone: (610) 593-1777; Fax: (610) 593-2002
E-mail: Info@schifferbooks.com

For the largest selection of fine reference books on this and related subjects, please visit our web site at
www.schifferbooks.com
We are always looking for people to write books on new and related subjects. If you have an idea for a book please contact us at the above address.

This book may be purchased from the publisher.
Include $5.00 for shipping.
Please try your bookstore first.
You may write for a free catalog.

In Europe, Schiffer books are distributed by
Bushwood Books
6 Marksbury Ave.
Kew Gardens
Surrey TW9 4JF England
Phone: 44 (0) 20 8392 8585; Fax: 44 (0) 20 8392 9876
E-mail: info@bushwoodbooks.co.uk
Website: www.bushwoodbooks.co.uk

contents

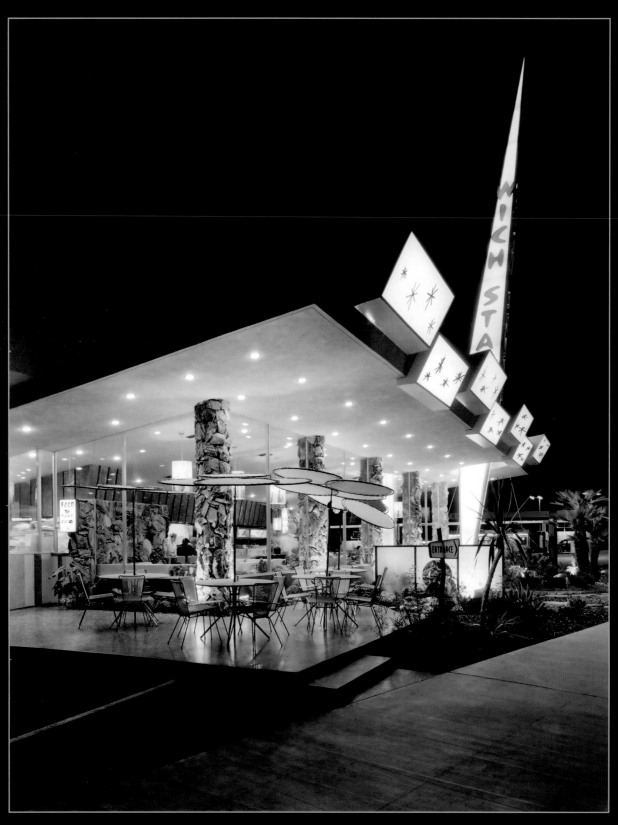

The Wich Stand, Inglewood, 1957, Armet + Davis, architects. *Photo: Jack Laxer.*

In viewing the work of fine architectural photographers many persons may naively infer that the photographers were fortunate to find all the elements in place when they composed their pictures to achieve the most realistic, dramatic effect. Nothing could be farther from the truth, as the following reminiscences illustrate.

As I peruse the various dining establishments in *Southern California Eats*, these pictures bring back nostalgic memories of my 40-plus years in architectural and travel photography.

A substantial portion of photography had to be done between the morning hours of 1 to 5 a.m. when there were no – or just a few – customers. This time-frame allowed me freedom to accessorize each of the many tables and counter settings with hundreds of items: i.e., glasses of water, napkins, silverware, menu and colored drinks (the latter added visual interest and depth).

In black/white photography, manipulation of the processed enlargement in the darkroom – via dodging, burning-in, flashing and brush-applied warm developer to appropriate areas – would help bring the inherent extreme lighting contrast of the scene to a latitude compatible with the relatively narrow latitude of the enlarging paper.

However, with color transparency photography, I used a pair of walkie-talkies to communicate and instruct my assistant to turn the bright neon sign off at the fuse/switch box for a number of seconds while the rest of the scene – which needed more exposure because it was relatively less bright than the sign – recorded itself on the film. Mother nature isn't always as thoughtful toward architectural photographers as we would like her to be. Trees, with their overhanging branches and leaves that help create dramatic framing for building exteriors, are often absent from prime composed views. After running into this frustrating situation a number of times early in my career, I designed a special boom and clamp (both infinitely adjustable) that attaches to my tripod and camera. This clamp holds various real and artificial branches (the latter are part of my equipment) which are lowered into precise position, thus dramatically framing the building.

In eliminating extraneous elements from scenes that would detract from the main subject, I am reminded of shooting the Los Angeles Music Center for Welton Becket while it was under construction. After composing the main building perfectly, I noticed a portable toilet off to the side – but impinging on an important portion of the scene. I asked the Construction Foreman if he could move the 'porta-potty' out of the way until I finished the picture. He promptly ordered one of his men to get a lift-truck and transport the toilet away. As the operator placed the forks of the lift under the toilet and elevated it, the toilet door suddenly swung open in mid-air and there stood a man quickly pulling up his pants while looking completely astonished and embarrassed. All witnesses will never forget that startling moment. At the time 'OCCUPADO' signs were not incorporated into the porta-potty design. The only person knowing it was occupied was the person inside.

Aside from all the unintentional embarrassment caused, I came up with splendid photographs – and a singular experience etched in my memory.

I trust my reminiscences provide information that enhances your appreciation for the photographic efforts of Adriene and John in producing *Southern California Eats*.

Cordially,

Jack Laxer

Jack Laxer
Architectural/Travel Photographer

Jack Laxer photographing a hotel lounge with his 3-D camera, San Diego, 2007.

Adriene was born in Hollywood, California and grew up living the slogan "See the USA in a Chevrolet." Every weekend, her Dad would pack the family into one of their many classic cars and set out on an exciting back road adventure. A typical Saturday might be a drive to Hadley's Orchards (a 200-mile round trip from their home in Tujunga) just to enjoy a date shake. And then, since they're just around the bend, why not visit the Cabazon dinosaurs?

In contrast, John grew up in New York City where his parents ran a local deli that was open every day except Mondays. His most extravagant excursion was a Saturday trip to Coney Island or Rockaway Beach with his older brothers when it reached 110 degrees in the swampy summers. If he saw one movie a year, it was a good year.

For years our favorite pastime has been weekend trips to find unusual, quirky, Southern California places. Throughout these trips, we became fascinated by the eateries we encountered. Whether they were restaurants, coffee shops, diners, cafeterias, drive-ins, drive-thrus, pizza parlors, ice cream parlors, or the less savory holes-in-the-walls, greasy spoons, burger joints, hot dog stands, it didn't matter; there was always

Top left: Adriene's dad, fresh from Brooklyn, NY. Tujunga, 1957. *Courtesy of John Biondo.*
Center left: Adriene hypnotizing her parakeet in her first car. Tujunga, 1958. *Courtesy of John Biondo.*
Top right: Adriene and her brother John on a family road trip, 1962. *Courtesy of John Biondo.*
Center right: Adriene riding a fiberglass horse, Carson City, 1962. *Courtesy of John Biondo.*
Bottom right: Adriene trying archery at a roadside motel, 1962. *Courtesy of John Biondo.*

11

something interesting about them, their history, the atmosphere, the people, the architecture.

When we started *Southern California Eats* we focused on the more unusual, zany, or under- appreciated haunts that have somehow slipped through the cracks. Not quite TOADS (Temporary, Obsolete, Abandoned, Derelict Sites), but more like FLODOS (Funky, Local, Overlooked, Destroyed Odd Structures or Forgotten, Low-brow, Off- the-Beaten-Track, Demolished, Oddball Sites). But after a bit more thought, we decided that by not including some of the well known classic Angeleno eateries like Musso & Frank's, Philippe's, and Apple Pan, we would not only alienate our audience but perform a disservice.

With such diversity you may wonder how we made our choices. First, to include every funky or historical eatery in Southern California would be impossible. We didn't even try. Second, just defining the boundaries was challenging. So we decided on everything below a line drawn across San Luis Obispo, Fresno, and Bishop. Then deciding *which* eatery to include in this book was much more difficult. They're all uniquely different, from architectural designs to fanciful themes, to those with historical and cultural significance. There's also a limit to how many can be included in one volume. We want to remind people who know these places that they're still around. For those who don't know, we want them to go and experience them firsthand. Once these time capsules are gone, they're gone. Uniquely American, we're among the last to experience these treasures.

13

Apple Pan

10801 Pico Boulevard, Los Angeles

At Apple Pan, the food, atmosphere and people instantly transports you back to Raymond Chandler's 1940s Los Angeles. We smelled this place a full block away. The food is excellent and there's plenty of it. Their hickory burgers are legendary and the ham and cheese sandwiches are not far behind. Apple Pan uses Tillamook cheddar with old school relish and pies à la mode, straight out of the Automat.

This family-owned restaurant started in 1947. Martha Gamble, the present owner, turned down big money for her property during the 1990s when the neighborhood was under heavy development. Her parents, Alan and Ellen, were the original owners and the recipes were handed down from her grandmother and other family members dating back to 1881.

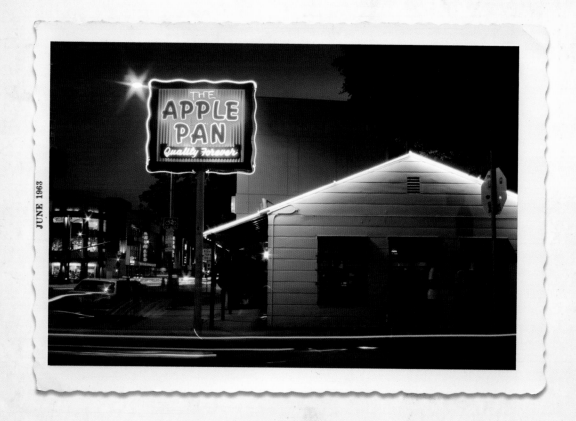

Gordon, still cheerfully taking orders in his forty-fourth year.

This eating establishment is housed in a small colonial, farm style building with a single U-shaped counter and 26 stools -- that's it, no tables, no booths. Apple Pan's semi-exhibition style kitchen sits in the center of the room, on top of the concrete floor. The neon sign outside is perfectly maintained: "Apple Pan Quality Forever." Our waiter, Gordon, has worked there 44 years; Charlie, the daytime cook, 51 years; and Isaac, the bus boy and junior of the group, only 30 years. Apple Pan...always a line, always worth the wait!

AMF Beverly Lanes (formerly Beverly Bowl)
1201 W. Beverly Boulevard, Montebello

Once home to a stunning neon sign now replaced with dull, standardized backlit plastic, this bowling alley is still worth the trip! Make your first stop the mysterious Masquerade Room. Chances are, the feisty bartender will regale you with amusing bowling stories while pouring you a Manhattan. Enjoy it in a dark booth under the gaze of the ever-delightful masquerade ball figures. These are not your run-of-the-mill wall decorations, they're like "It's A Small World" on acid. Mary Blair and Jim Flora would've loved them for their obtuse and silly take. After bowling a game or two, grab a slice of pizza at the coffee shop, a rare Case-Study, Eichleresque post-and-beam structure decked out with ball lights.

Bob's BIG BOY

4211 W. Riverside Drive, Toluca Lake/Burbank

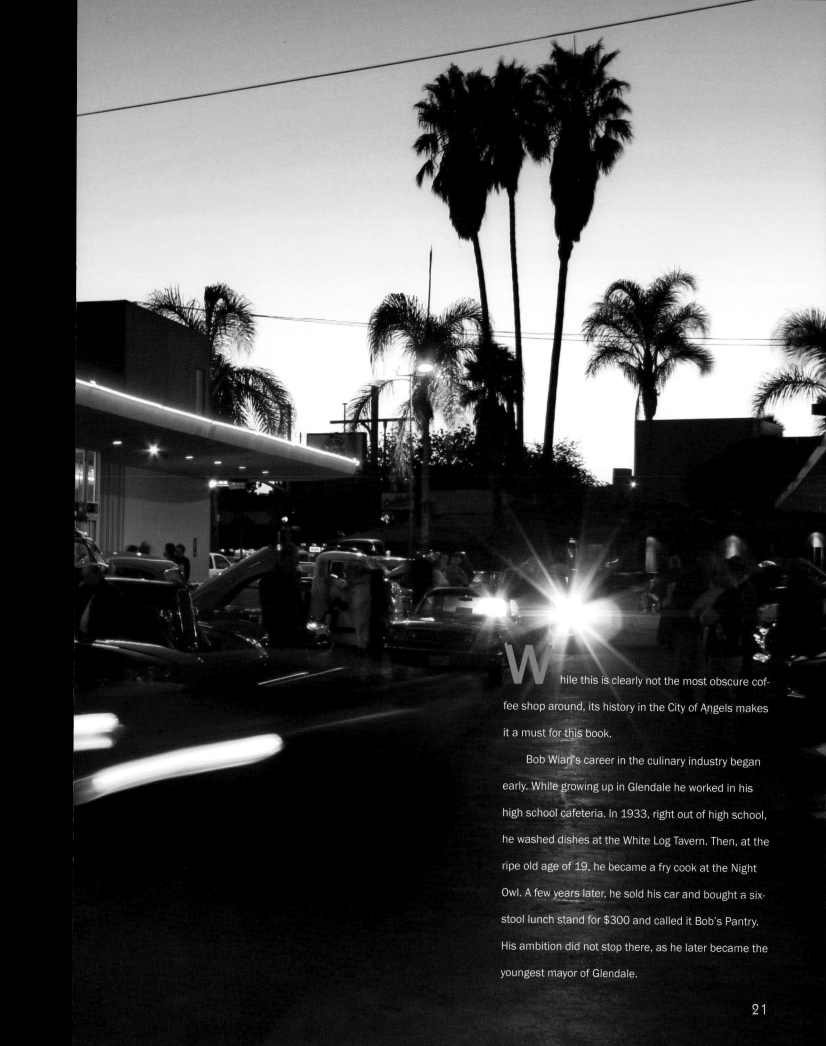

hile this is clearly not the most obscure coffee shop around, its history in the City of Angels makes it a must for this book.

Bob Wian's career in the culinary industry began early. While growing up in Glendale he worked in his high school cafeteria. In 1933, right out of high school, he washed dishes at the White Log Tavern. Then, at the ripe old age of 19, he became a fry cook at the Night Owl. A few years later, he sold his car and bought a six-stool lunch stand for $300 and called it Bob's Pantry. His ambition did not stop there, as he later became the youngest mayor of Glendale.

In 1949, Wian hired Wayne McAllister to design the Bob's Big Boy drive-in restaurant in Toluca Lake. The ever colorful McAllister was already a seasoned pro in casino and restaurant design by this time. Like Wian, McAllister started his career at a young age. Only a year after graduating from high school, while working as a draftsman at an architectural firm in San Diego, he was given the prize job of designing Agua Caliente, a prestigious resort in Tijuana, Mexico.

This Bob's Big Boy in Toluca Lake was threatened with demolition in the early 1990s, but an alarmed community, spearheaded by the L.A. Conservancy's Modern Committee and classic car enthusiasts, rallied together in support. In a tremendous victory, Bob's dodged the wrecking ball, was landmarked, and went on to become the highest grossing Big Boy in the chain. On Friday nights you'll find Bob's transformed into a classic car mecca, packed with hot rods, show cars, and, if you're lucky, the amphibious Amphicar.

Wedding reception by the Agua Caliente pool. Mexico, 2007.

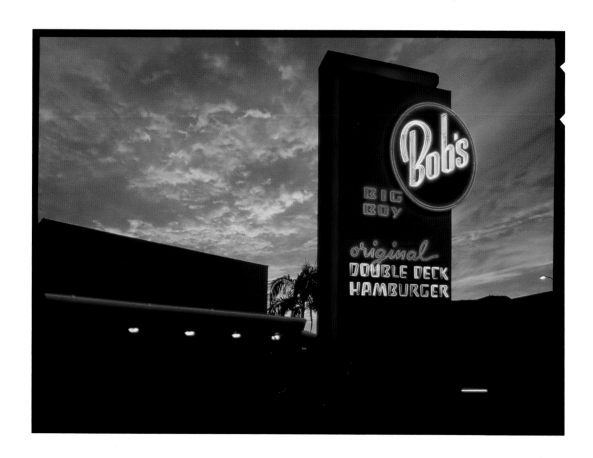

Opposing page:
Bandleader on break at Agua Caliente. Wedding of
Chris and Charlene Nichols, Tijuana, Mexico, 2007.

Bun 'n Burger
1000 E. Main Street, Alhambra

Take personal service, add a pre-World War II neon sign extravaganza, and you've got the historic Bun 'n Burger. Cruise down Main Street at dusk to catch the neon chef in action. The custom corner building was designed in 1940 by architect Walter Zick. The enormous dining room was formerly an insurance office, later annexed by the original diner. It now doubles as a charming museum of antiques and photos of the old San Gabriel Valley. Owners Alicia and Arturo Sanchez nurture a loyal following of regulars.

CHICKEN PIE SHOP & **BAKERY**

928 N Euclid Street La Palma

The city of Anaheim underwent massive development in the late 1950s and early 1960s as Disneyland attracted visitors from all over the world. Most of those atomic age restaurants, motels, and business buildings are now gone, but the shopping center housing this Chicken Pie Shop has somehow survived. The angled windows facing west recall the Mission Coffee Shop in Pomona. Next door, the barber shop with the boomerang shaped planter, steel deck canopy, and dual palm trees piercing the roofline (aka 'botanical breakthroughs') are classic elements of space-age Googie style. The Chicken Pie Shop is also a bakery and everything is freshly made in-house. It's good, fast, and cheap. What else could you ask for?

Ultra-futuristic monorail in Tomorrowland. Disneyland, Anaheim, 2004.

27

11908 Hawthorne Boulevard, Hawthorne

1957, architect Harry Harrison

Y*ou can't beat Chip's stunning Googie signage, a series of neon lit rooftop canisters spelling out the name C-H-I-P-S. Owner Manny Romero has done a fabulous job restoring Chip's and maintaining its classic Coffee Shop Modern style as designed by Harry Harrison in 1957. Chip's customers can also dine outdoors in the enclosed patio. Manny still serves up good old American food and hot coffee, just like in the old days. Rent Hollywoodland to catch a few scenes featuring Chip's. After enjoying Chip's, visit the nearby Pizza Show, Rustic Lite cocktail bar, Brolly Hut, or Nat's Coffee Shop at the Hawthorne Airport.*

Du-par's long history began in 1926 when 'Tiny' Naylor (who was well over six feet tall) opened Tiny's Waffle Shop in Fresno. Tiny's did so well that he opened a Du-par's restaurant in L.A.'s Farmer's Market in 1938. Using nothing but the freshest ingredients, Du-par's became known for their award-winning pies, baked right on the premises. And Du-par's Old Fashioned Buttermilk Hotcakes and Golden Brown French Toast are always favorites. Recently, their historic Farmers Market location was completely renovated. All three are still family owned and run by Tiny's son, Biff Naylor, and his daughter.

Eatz/Los Feliz Café
3207 Los Feliz Boulevard,
Atwater

Just east of the L.A. River, on the Los Feliz Municipal Golf Course is this delightful Quonset hut of a coffee shop. Eatz could be the sole surviving quonset of the World War II-era Rodger Young Village that once sprawled across Los Feliz along the river. Formerly Eatz, it is now the Los Feliz Café (not to be confused with the Café Los Feliz). Location scouts love it, and we can think of nowhere else in Los Angeles where you can dine in a quonset.

31

Evergreen Café
1269 Evergreen Road, Wrightwood

The village of Wrightwood boasts of having no malls and no street lights. It is located in the northeast end of the San Gabriel Mountains at 6000 feet above sea level. About eight miles east, just off the 15 (the main artery from Los Angeles to Las Vegas) are the picturesque 'Mormon Rocks' named after the Mormons who homesteaded in adjacent Lone Pine Canyon in 1851. If you spend more than five minutes in this area, a train will pass, immediately reminding you of an HO scale train set nestled in a miniature cyclorama. There is a surreal quality here that reminds us of Joshua Tree National Monument and the Alabama Hills in the Eastern Sierras. Since this is part of the Angeles National Forest, there are many recreational activities here, from fishing, water skiing, camping, and hiking, to skiing in the winter.

Evergreen Café has been open since the 1920s when L.A. County established a major recreational facility in Big Pines. This cafe, housed in a country log cabin style exterior, boasts friendly service inside its shabby chic 1980s interior.

Four 'n 20

5855 Van Nuys Boulevard, Van Nuys

This unique 1960s restaurant was designed in the shape of four stylized trees. While similar to Mary Blair's "Small World" in Disneyland, originally constructed for the 1964 New York World's Fair, this was an actual three-dimensional building that operated as a restaurant. Four 'N 20 started out in 1969 as a pie shop, later expanding to a full-service restaurant with vegetarian options. In 1998, this location was unceremoniously leveled to make room for a car lot. Van Nuys Boulevard was once the San Fernando Valley's premiere cruising boulevard, with drive-ins like Bob's Big Boy and Oscar's. Now they've all been replaced by auto dealerships.

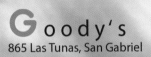

Goody's
865 Las Tunas, San Gabriel

"Graciously serving you since 1956." The industrial 'swiss cheese' I-beam supporting Goody's classic Googie sign is just awesome. Inside this diner, you'll find a modern ranch style similar to Rod's Grill in Arcadia. But here at Goody's, the waitresses still wear uniforms. Is it our imagination or does Salvador Rodriquez, the owner, look like the chef they adopted as their mascot?

GOODY'S

Harvey'sw/Johnie's Broiler
7447 E. Firestone Boulevard, Downey

On January 7, 2007, the late night news reported that a Downey landmark had been leveled. A wrecking crew had illegally bulldozed a 1958 landmark without even fencing off the property or turning off the electricity. This was Harvey's Broiler, once the heart and soul of Downey, and the Southland's ultimate car cruising destination. Harvey's carhops never wore roller skates, but with 350 parking spaces and 98 covered carhop spaces, they certainly could've used them.

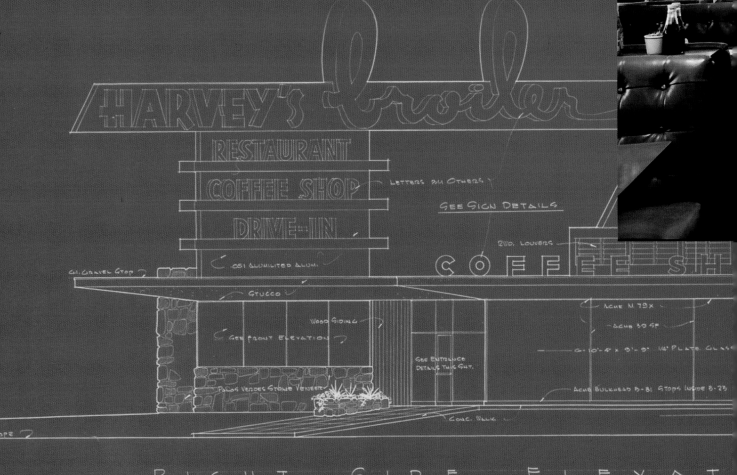

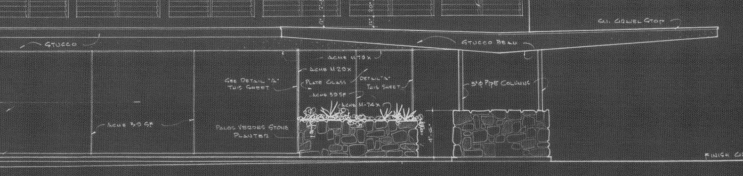

This was The Place to show off. Customs, deuces, hot rods, and lead sleds would jam Firestone Boulevard, all hoping for a chance to get in. Larry Watson, Ed "Big Daddy" Roth,... they all cruised here. And couples flirted, fell in love, and even got married at Harvey's.

To make a long story short, things were swell 'til Harvey Ortner became ill in the 1960s. Harvey's was renamed "Johnie's," and though cruise nights continued for awhile, in

A spunky 92 year old Minnie Ortner at the time the Broiler closed, 2002.

High school students at Harvey's Broiler, 1960s. *Courtesy of George Redfox.*

There were numerous rallies and car cruises in support of Johnie's Broiler.

Analisa Ridenour and Adriene, 2007.

time they were replaced by movie shoots for films like *License to Drive, Heat,* and *What's Love Got To Do With It.* By New Year's Eve 2001, it was all over. The Broiler was gutted and turned into a used car lot. A grass roots coalition took action, partnering with the Modern Committee to save the sign and secure the Broiler's eligibility on the State Register. The Friends kept watch over the sad sight of the decaying Broiler for six years, ultimately halting the 2007 demolition-in-progress. Following the destruction, they created the Coalition to Rebuild the Broiler and organized rallies and 'ghost cruises' to keep the Broiler alive in the news.

In early 2008, things finally turned around. Bob's Big Boy franchise operator Jim Louder signed a long-term lease and announced plans to reconstruct the historic drive-in and restaurant. Using Paul Clayton's original 1958 blueprints, a newly revamped "Bob's Big Boy Broiler" is scheduled to open in 2009. And we can't wait.

J's/Catalina's Coffee Shop
250 E. Highland Avenue, San Bernardino

In 2004, we had a long conversation with Yvonne, who was the owner of J's in San Bernardino. She was one of the original waitresses at Mr Foxy's just a couple of miles west on Highland Avenue, the first of a chain of A-framed restaurants owned by Burt Richardson. Yvonne told us that after WWII, Richardson worked at the Magic Lamp on Route 66 before opening Mr Foxy's with a couple of buddies in the mid 1950s. Pretty soon, they had a chain of six Foxy's throughout the Southland. These restaurants were loosely based on the Chalets of Switzerland and most (not all) were A-frame buildings.

Former Mr Foxy waitress Yvonne owned
and operated J's until early 2000.

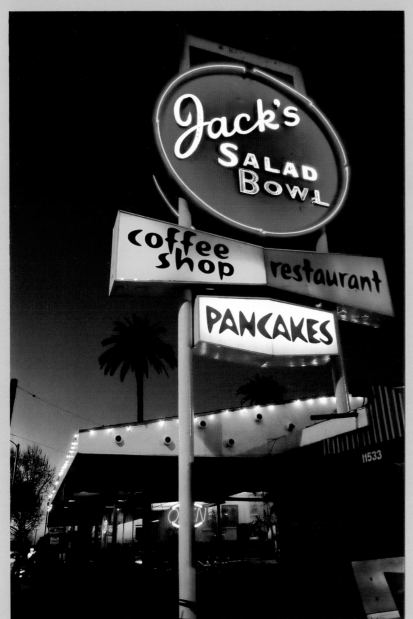

Jack's Salad Bowl
1527 Whittier Boulevard, Whittier

From the architect who designed Ships in Westwood (demo'd in 1983) and Ships in Culver City (now a Starbucks), this 1957-58 Googie style Coffee Shop has seen better days. It has gone through multiple owners who systematically stripped away just about all the unique qualities this coffee shop once had.

Originally from New York, architect Martin Stern, Jr. moved to Los Angeles in the 1930s and had worked for the movie studios and other architects such as Paul R. Williams, before designing apartment buildings, tract housing, bowling alleys, shopping centers, and coffee shops on his own. In Las Vegas, he is generally recognized as the one responsible for turning a low-rise sprawl into a hi-rise metropolis with his concepts of casino structural integration.

JOHNIE'S

COFFEE SHOP + RESTAURANT

6101 Wilshire Boulevard, Los Angeles

An early classic from Louis Armet and Eldon Davis, this restaurant started out as Romeo's Times Square in 1955. Located on the southwest corner of Wilshire Boulevard and Fairfax, across the street from the Moderne monument May Company, Romeo's featured a butterfly roof as well as flickering incandescent light bulbs and neon signage. Shortly after opening, it changed to Ram's, then to Johnie's. A superb Googie representation, Johnie's is often used prominently in movies such as *Miracle Mile* and *Volcano*. Sadly, Johnie's closed its restaurant doors for good in June 2000 when the neighboring owner of the 99 Cents Only Store bought the property for its parking spaces.

Little Red Hen Coffee Shop
2697 N. Fair Oaks Avenue, Altadena

When we stopped in, Lonzia Shay was making himself a sandwich and watching "'I Love Lucy" on a funky red TV that fit his place like a glove. Lonzia moved to Pasadena with his family from Mississippi when he was 22. His mother, Rena, bought the restaurant around 1973 from a woman named Doris. The counter and equipment was moved in from another location. The tiny café seats approximately 18 (mostly along the L-shaped counter) so any time we've stopped in it's been SRO at the LRH. Six telling photos taped to the wall outline their heroes: Nat King Cole, Aretha Franklin, Billie Holiday, Cassius Clay, James Brown, and Sam Cooke. Custom red and white key rings decorate the wall, and Adriene smiled when Lonzia told her to take one for her '56 Oldsmobile.

"I just like cooking" says Lonzia, "it's been always my thing since I was 19…it's a small place, and there's one cook, and everybody wants their food at one time. And I have like 15 orders in and 26 people waiting – it gets hectic." A customer favorite is the 'shipwrecked egg,' for those who like their eggs scrambled hard.

Lonzia spreading the gospel of hard work. "You can make a decent living if you're willing to work hard, just look at me...."

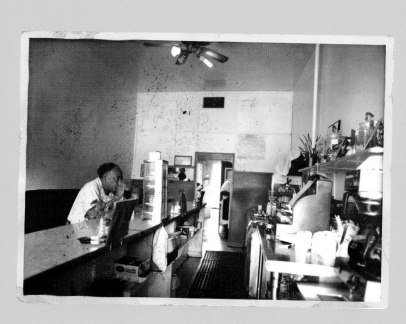

Vintage pictures. *Courtesy of Lonzia Shay.*

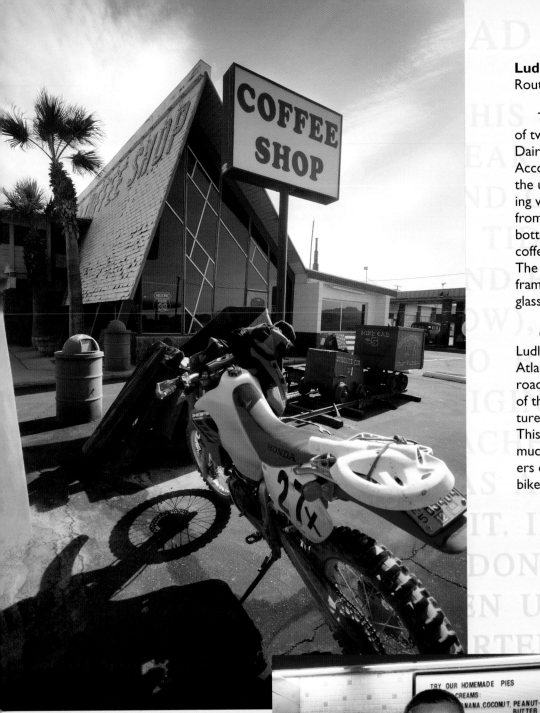

Ludlow Coffee Shop
Route 66, Ludlow

The town of Ludlow consists of two gas stations, a motel, a Dairy Queen, and this coffee shop. According to our waiter, Charlie, the upper two-thirds of this building was an old church moved here from the town of Bishop while the bottom one-third was an existing coffee shop made of cinder blocks. The roof is an *asymmetrical* A-frame structure with resin/stained glass.

Originally founded in 1882, Ludlow was a water stop for the Atlantic and Central Pacific Railroad. Since it's smack in the middle of the Mojave Desert, the temperature often runs into triple digits. This Route 66 town still provides a much-welcomed rest stop to travelers of Highway 40 and weekend dirt bike enthusiasts.

Our waiter, Charlie, was very knowledgeable about the Mojave Desert region.

Mission Family Restaurant
888 W. Mission Boulevard, Pomona

This 1958 Googie-style coffee shop may very well be the last intact postwar modern coffee shop in all of Pomona. Once home to many, Pomona's double butterfly IHOP and a pre-Kroc McDonalds are now gone, ditto for Van de Kamp's windmill and original Googie-style Denny's which has been altered beyond recognition. We're always happy to stop in for a friendly breakfast at the Mission (they've got good reviews). It gives us a chance to admire the sculpted architectural tiles and volcanic stone near the front entry. You can still see "HH" imbedded in the tile, which goes back to its origins as Hull House restaurant.

NORDIC FOX/ FOXY'S

10924 Paramount Boulevard, Downey

Opened in 1968 as Foxy's, the Nordic Fox served Swedish food Viking style. This unique A-frame building has three miles of rope cleverly concealing the central HVAC duct system. The restaurant's northeast wall is embedded with real cut logs, and

triangular fireplaces bookend both ends of the build-

ing. The backs of the counter seats are molded wood

with astrological symbols and can be removed to cre-

ate a buffet. Door handles to the main entrance are

actual ice axes from the 1960s. Out front there was

once a modern sculpture of a fox with a long neck, but a

customer recalled watching a former owner removing it

with a hatchet, and no one has seen it since. In mid 2008,

Nordic Fox switched owners and now operates as the

Downey Brewing Co.

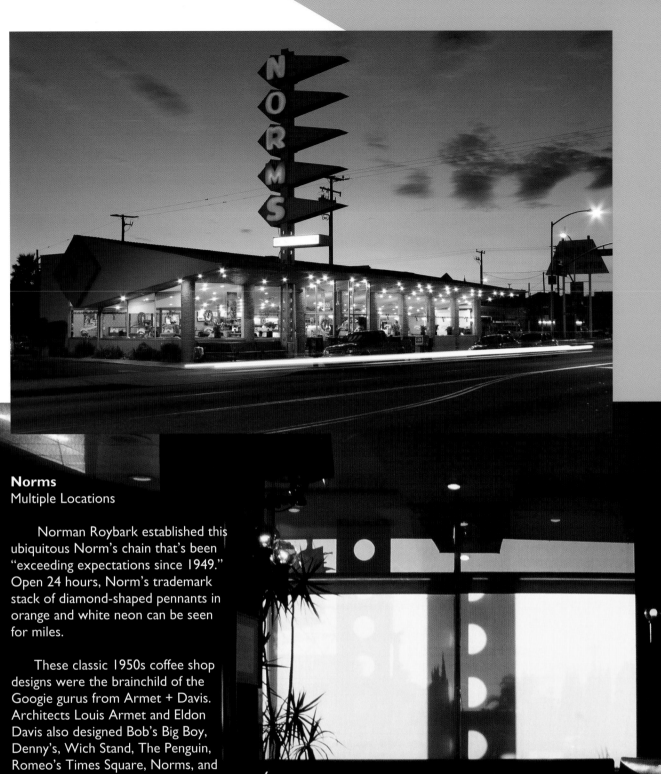

Norms
Multiple Locations

Norman Roybark established this ubiquitous Norm's chain that's been "exceeding expectations since 1949." Open 24 hours, Norm's trademark stack of diamond-shaped pennants in orange and white neon can be seen for miles.

These classic 1950s coffee shop designs were the brainchild of the Googie gurus from Armet + Davis. Architects Louis Armet and Eldon Davis also designed Bob's Big Boy, Denny's, Wich Stand, The Penguin, Romeo's Times Square, Norms, and Tiny Naylor's. Innovators of the post-war California Coffee Shop Modern style, they were also experts at

dling the vocabulary of tropical, Polynesian, and Asian themes like the Kon Tiki in Riverside.

Armet and Davis both graduated from USC's School of Architecture. Frank Lloyd Wright and Richard Neutra were significant influences, as was instructor Whitney Smith. Armet + Davis pioneered the use of flagcrete, web-steel I-beams, floor to ceiling glass, and integrated signage, which served both structural and visual (advertising) purposes.

Restaurant equipment designer Stan Abrams brought semi-exhibition cooking, cantilevered seating, and Herman Miller-Eames designed furniture to the mix. Architect Helen Fong supervised the various projects, including Pann's. Lee Linton, a maverick designer, produced dynamic and flamboyant renderings that sold the exuberance of the design concepts.

Pann's
6710 La Tijera Boulevard, Ladera Heights

Standing in a triangular island between LaTijera at LaCienega and Cen-
tinela Boulevard, Pann's is arguably
the best representation of an original
Googie-style coffee shop in Los Angeles.
George and Rena Panagopoulos had a
dream of moving to California and own-
ing a successful business. George was a
Greek immigrant who enlisted in the U.S.
Air Force during WW II. He was sent to
Italy where he cooked in the field for the
U.S. troops and generals. When he
returned to the States, George

cooked at the Pantry in North Hollywood before opening Rena's Café in the heart of Inglewood. In 1958, George and Rena fulfilled their dream by hiring Armet + Davis to design their ultra-modern restaurant, Pann's. It's still family owned and run by their son, Jim. Don't forget to try their 'sock-it-to-me' cake, it's *faaantastic*!

Our pal Jay Falconer at Pann's: a die-hard Punker turned special education instructor.

The Parasol
12241 Seal Beach, Los Alamitos

While still in high school, Roy Hall found himself managing an A-frame Huddle Hut restaurant in Idaho when the older manager quit and walked off one day. Roy later moved to Southern California and began managing the first Parasol in Torrance for Angelo Pappas in 1961 (demo'd in the 1990s). A few years later, Roy began to manage the Parasol in Seal Beach, which he later bought. This unique parasol building included custom parasol lighting fixtures and a central core refrigeration system that was the hub of the operation.

The 1967 Parasol in Seal Beach, designed by
architect Charles Kanner, was one of the most intact
programmatic restaurants in the entire Los Angeles
area, that is until 2005 when redevelopment plans
were announced for the shopping center. A local
grass roots effort to save The Parasol was formed.
When the developers became aware that over
15,000 signatures were gathered to preserve the
dome-shaped building, they came to their senses and
decided *against* demolition.

Good Morning!

Breakfast

FRUITS AND JUICES

...ge Juice	
...ice, Slice Lemon	20-35
... Juice	20-35
...Pineapple	20-35
... Prunes	35
...	35
... Beauty Apple (in Season)	35
...without Cream)	35
...t	50
...	35

Chef's Special
GOLDEN BROWN
BUTTERMILK HOT CAKES
with Maple Syrup
One Fresh Ranch Egg
Choice of Ham, Bacon or Sausage
$1.05

HOT OR COLD CEREALS (Served with Cream) 35c

...ND EGGS
...E AND EGGS
...GER PATTIES OR
...UT PORK CHOP
...GGS

Toast and Jelly
with or without
Hashed Browned
Potatoes
$1.35

PANCAKE SANDWICH 85c
Golden Brown Buttermilk Hot Cakes,
Two Fresh Ranch Eggs with
Maple Syrup and
Pure Creamery Butter

...TOP
...STEAK
...Ranch Eggs
... Potatoes
...Jelly

GOLDEN BROWN BUTTERMILK HOT CAKES 60c
BLUEBERRY HOT CAKES 70c
Made from Our Own Recipe of the Finest Ingredients
Served with Maple Syrup and Pure Butter

...otatoes, Toast and Jelly 65   TWO EGGS, Potatoes, Toast and Jelly 75
FRENCH TOAST with Maple Syrup   85

...der of Bacon or Sausage 65   Toasted English Muffin
...er Fried Ham   65   with Jelly
...der of Two   Doughnuts (Each)   25
...urger Patties   Toast and Jelly   10
...er of Two Fried Eggs   65   Cinnamon Toast   20
...in   50   Coffee Cake   25
                          20   25

— OPEN 24 HOURS —

...staurant   coffee shop

LOCATED:

...Coast Highway   12241 Los Alamitos
...renshaw Blvd.   Rossmoor Shopping Center
...California   Los Alamitos, California
...4220   598-3311

THE PARASOL

restaurant

coffee shop

The Parasol under renovation in 2007, reminiscent of a carousel minus the animals.

Pioneer Town Bowl
53613 Mane Street, Yucca Valley

What's a 1960s bowling alley doing out here in the middle of nowhere? We soon learned that we were in Pioneertown, named after the Sons of the Pioneers. Built in 1946 by investors who envisioned a circa 1870 Frontier movie set, complete with their favorite pastimes...drinking and bowling. After strolling through town, we ended up at Lane #1, where Roy Rogers bowled Pioneer's very first ball, a strike! The lanes were renovated in the

1960s, and there they've stayed, frozen in time. After a few games, we ordered sandwiches at the counter. An aging ex-dance hall girl treated us to sarsparilla (she doubles on weekends during Pioneertown's free Cowboy Reenactments). Complete with a motel, restaurant, stables, and bowling alley, this is a detour certainly worth taking!

PIONEER TOWN

Roy's Café
Route 66, Amboy

Over decades of happy motoring, Route 66 has been elevated into mythic status. Songs, books, and even a popular TV show have been based on this famous highway. Amboy was a major stop on the Mother Road between Chicago and Santa Monica until the 1970s when Interstate 40 bypassed this town completely. The Amboy community includes Roy's Café, which is actually in the gas station, a post office, church, school, and a 1959 Googie motel with Roy's world famous neon sign! In 2005, Albert Okura of the Juan Pollo chain bought the entire town and 500 acres (no mule) after a failed auction on eBay. Okura is restoring the town, starting with the gas station, which opened to terrific fanfare in April 2008.

The Saugus Cafe
25861 San Fernando Road, Saugus

Their card reads: "The Original Saugus Café. The oldest restaurant in L.A. County. Established 1886. Open 24 hours." Currently owned by Alfredo Mercado, its long and illustrious history began on September 1, 1887 when Joseph Herbert Tolfree opened the restaurant on the north end of the Mojave Train Station. President Benjamin Harrison ate here during his re-election campaign. President Theodore Roosevelt visited in May 1903. In 1904, William Mulholland, the Chief of Los Angeles Department of Water and Power, stopped in for breakfast with Mayor Fred Eaton.

Around 1916, film productions discovered this versatile location and D.W. Griffith, John Ford, Douglas Fairbanks, Mary Pickford, Charlie Chaplin, and William S. Hart became frequent guests. Later, Clark Gable, Gary Cooper, John Wayne, and Tom Mix visited. In 1953, the Saugus Café appeared in Frank Sinatra *Suddenly* with Sterling Hayden.

Ships
Multiple Locations: Westwood, Culver City, Los Angeles

The 1984 destruction of this ultra-modern coffee shop in Westwood galvanized a modern preservation movement with the creation the Modern Committee by the Los Angeles Conservancy. Twenty-four years later, Modcom still works passionately to preserve modern historical buildings such as Hollywood's Capitol Records tower, Driftwood Dairy, Holiday Bowl, and Johnie's Broiler. Although Ships is gone, somehow just glancing at pictures of it brings back the feelings of hope and unlimited possibilities of the postwar period.

Summit Inn Café
Off the Oak Hill exit of Interstate 15, Cajon Pass

Their signs read: "Historic Summit Inn Cafe since 1952, Route 66, date shakes and ostrich burgers locally grown by OK Corral Ostrich Farm." This place is on the Cajon Pass, elevation 4257, just off the 15 between San Bernardino and Victorville towards Las Vegas. The outside is littered with shells of old vehicles along with mining equipment and gas pumps. Make no mistake, this is a classy joint. Where else can you find your choice of Glow-Ons, Temptation, Pandora's Box, and Extenders for just 50 cents, not to mention three choices of men's cologne for only 25 cents each, all in one place: the men's room. Elvis even stopped here. There's everything you'd expect from a Route 66 roadside tourist trap: deer trophies, restored gas pumps, vintage pictures of the cafe in the '50s, a '70s jukebox, a gift shop, and the One Penny Fortune Telling Machine. Don't forget the Ostrich Burgers, they're supposed to taste like chicken.

WAGON WHEEL BOWLING
2801 Wagon Wheel Road, Oxnard

Currently threatened with extinction for
a trio of proposed high-rise towers (hard to
believe we still need more of these), Wagon
Wheel Junction put the little town of Oxnard on
the map. A destination for travelers since 1947,
this complex was the first project from Oxnard's
premiere developer, Martin V. "Bud" Smith. This
1953 bowling alley was designed by Beverly Hills
architect Arthur Froehlich, known for his race-

track designs for Hollywood Park, Belmont, and world famous Hanna-Barbera cartoon studios.

Originally named Hoberg's in honor of proprietor Ed Hoberg, the bowling alley's cafe still feeds hungry bowling leagues. The café floor is covered with red linoleum rarely seen and some of the seats have been repaired so much that you're not sure if they're covered in red naugahyde or red duct tape. It doesn't matter; this place has character, history, and soul.

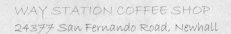

This corner coffee shop opened in 1971 in the small rural town of Newhall. We learned that the stools were brought here from Fillmore, an old railroad town some 25 miles west. The counter is covered in 1970s floor linoleum with a real 'Ask The Swami' fortune telling machine. It's similar to the one in the "Twilight Zone" episode "Nick of Time", where a young William Shatner became so obsessed by the fortune telling machine that he almost lost the ability to make decisions for himself.

Zingo's Café
3201 Buck Owens Boulevard, Bakersfield

This 24/7, seat yourself truck stop has been here since the 1950s and participates in Bakersfield's Fabulous Fifties Car Show. You can find the 'love kits' they sell in their men's room on eBay. Apparently for only 75 cents (if you buy them from the men's room here) you not only get full protection, but an illustrated *manual* on the various love positions that are possible using these pleasure-giving devices. Guess it's all part of roadside Americana.

BBQ

CHILI JOINTS

Cafe

Restaurants

PIZZA

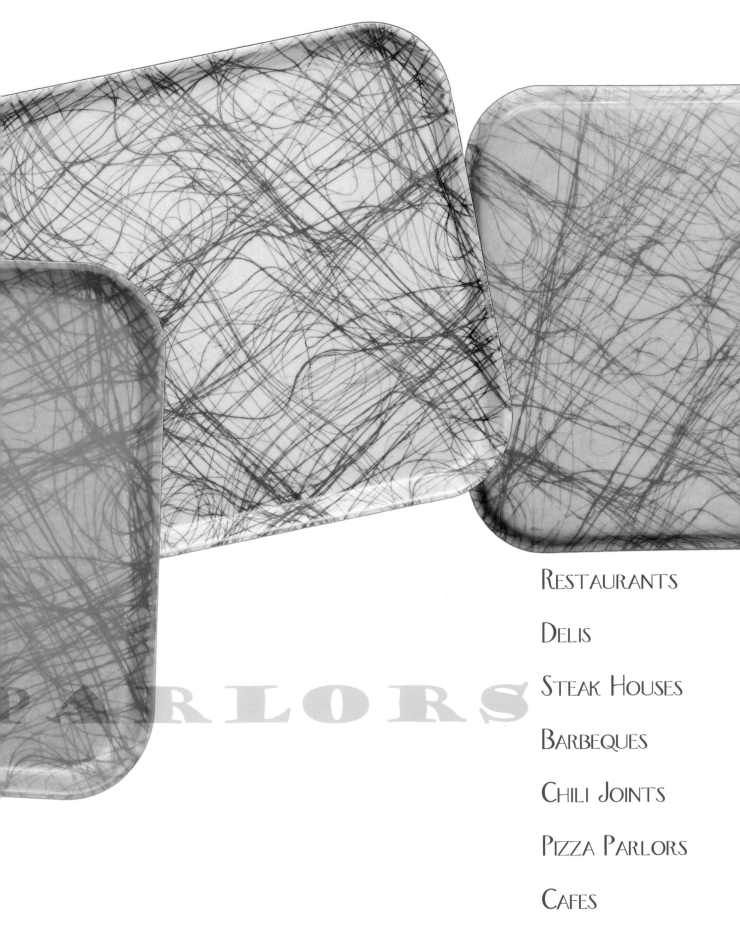

PARLORS

RESTAURANTS

DELIS

STEAK HOUSES

BARBEQUES

CHILI JOINTS

PIZZA PARLORS

CAFES

Arturo's
25720 Western Avenue, Lomita

Just north of the Pacific Coast Highway, this elegant restaurant is circa 1960s. Unlike any other Mexican restaurant we've been to, this mid-century modern building is as close to an Eichler house (or Case Study House, for that matter) as you can get. It has posts and beams, floor-to-ceiling glass, a flat roof, grooved wood panels, ball lights, and even an atrium. The drop-down cocktail bar toward the rear is so cool you totally expect to see Matt Helm shmoozing Ann Margaret as you approach. The food is authentic and excellent. This restaurant is still owned and run by the original family that commissioned its construction. Go, see, and enjoy.

79

Aztec Hotel/Mayan Bar and Grill
311 W. Foothill Boulevard, Monrovia

This surreal 1925 masterpiece sits on an early alignment of the Mother Road that pre-dates Route 66. It was designed by eccentric British architect-adventurer Robert B. Stacy-Judd, a real-life Indiana Jones with an obsession for Pre-Columbian/Meso-American archeology. After two expeditions to Mexico, he wrote three books on the Mayan Culture. He also designed the Soboba Hot Springs and Atwater Bungalows. Aztec's historic hideaway's guest list includes Jack Benny and other celebrities who frequented nearby Santa Anita Racetrack. During the Depression, the hotel was hit so hard it doubled as a speakeasy and bordello.

Aztec's present owner, Kathie Reese-McNeill, is devoted to breathing life back into this National Register treasure. And with family Sundays, Taco Tuesdays, live music seven days a week, an art gallery, barber shop, and live parakeets in the main lobby, the Aztec is well on its way. In the Mayan Room, organist Jim McEwan plays everything from Sinatra to Mario Lanza when not accompanying the loyal singers who date back to his Trails and El Encanto days. It's a must for those into the low-brow, kooky fringe culture of Los Angeles.

Luncheon Menu

substitutions.

...TION 7.25
...: Beef, ham or pastrami, accompanied with
...course a slice of fresh pineapple

...CH 4.95
...e of ham, beef or pastrami, zesty barbeque
... salad and of course a slice of fresh pineapple

.... 5.45
... Served with piping hot homemade soup and
... extra

.... 4.25
..., served with homemade cole slaw or a small

.... 4.95
...celery and bell peppers. Served with

.... 5.40
...grilled on sourdough accompanied by a small

.... 5.65
... French roll with your choice of fries or corn
...aw

.... 4.95
...ed with melted cheese, served with Fries and a salad
...uest

.... 5.75
...chili, topped with melted cheese, fries and a salad or

.... 4.95
...WICH
...and bell pepper. Served on wheat, sourdough or a
...slaw

.... 4.95
...se and olives, chopped onions on request

.... 4.35
...CH
...rami and cheese. Piled h...

...H
...arbeque sauce, piled high...
...your choice of cole slaw

...r liking on a slice of so...
...alad or cole slaw

...own, topped with a slice...
...salad or cole slaw

...HEESE ....
...se, grilled on
...aw or salad

...ders

...... Cup 1.5...

.... 1.9...
.... 1.75
... 2.25 Bowl 3.95
.... 1.25
.... 3.25

... checks please

... N. Rosemead Blvd.
...emead, CA 91770
...818) 285-1241

...ject to Change Without Notice

... SALAD ....(Large) 1.50
... SLICED PINEAPPLE 1.95
... CHOWDER 1.75
... GE CHEESE (1 Scoop) ...... Cup 2.50 Bowl 4.25
... POTATO 1.25
.... 2.50

Beverages

...REWED DECAFFEINATED 1.00
...ROUND COFFEE 1.00
...EWED ICED TEA 1.00
...LATE 1.00
... DIET SODA 1.50
... MINERAL WATER 1.25
... SODA 1.25
... MILK 1.25

FRIED FILET OF FISH 4.50
FRIED FILET OF FISH 4.25

We Accept ONLY MasterCard, Visa, Discover, Diner's Club, Carte Blanche

.95
.95
.75

4.25
3.75

2.75
.50

95

#3

#4 BA...
   s...

#5 TER...
   ½...
   slo...

#6 GOL...
   Ligh...

#7 GOL...
   A ger...

#8 TERIY...
   A delic...
   Bahook...

#9 TERIYA...
   STUFF...
   For tho...
   and delic...

82

BAHOOKA Ribs & Grog
4501 N. Rosemead Boulevard, Rosemead

Bahooka means "shack" in Hawaiian, and what a shack it is! Assembling the Bahooka by hand and decorating it with salvaged naval equipment, this shipwreck of a restaurant began in 1967 when Jack Fliegel (a WWII Navy vet and Kelbo's bartender) envisioned converting the former restaurant on the site to a Polynesian-style restaurant. Where else can you go and be greeted by fishes in over a hundred aquariums? Even the counter at the bar is a fish tank. Our pal Rufus is a twenty-something fish with the distinction of being a star! A large, 34 pound Pacu with an attitude, he puts on a show by eating carrots. Johnny Depp starred with Rufus in the 1997 feature film *Fear and Loathing in Las Vegas* and with Jim Carrey in *The Number 23*. According to the Bahooka's website, in a rare interview, Rufus said, "I like carrots, kids, and good looking women," not necessarily in that order.

83

Sunrise at the Bahooka. Vintage 1934 Woody. *Car courtesy of Kevin Preciado.* Top right: Rufus posing with a carrot in his mouth, like a cigar.

Bear Pit (originally Baier Pit)
10825 Sepulveda Boulevard, Mission Hills

Ben Baier opened his first barbecue in a shack attached to a church in Newhall. He developed his special recipes from his Kansas City, Missouri background and became known for Missouri Style wood smoked meat with the Baier Pit's secret BBQ sauce. Later, he partnered with Don Carrow of Carrow's Restaurant chain and opened the Baier Pit in Mission Hills in the 1950s. Country western singer Tennessee Ernie Ford endorsed their food. It then expanded and changed ownership several times, eventually becoming the Bear Pit we know today, complete with Tiki torches, murals of bears (rumored to have been painted by Disney animators), and lots of sawdust on the floors.

CHEF'S SALAD
Crisp Fresh Garden Greens Mixed
Julienne Ham, Chee___, Hard Boiled Egg,
Wedges, and Our D___ ___ Boiled Toast 7.75

GRILLED CHICKEN SALAD
Boneless and Skin___ ___ Breast of Chicken
on Bed of Crisp Green ___
and Honey Sesame Dressing

TUNA SALAD
Generous Portions of Delic___ ___ ___ surrounded
by Tomato W___ ___ on a Crisp Bed of ___
with a Quarter ___ ___ Egg 6.75

SMALL TUNA SALAD
DINNER SALAD
Choice of Dressing

KNOCKWURST ___
___ with Our Famous Ba___
___ ___ and Garlic Toast

CHILI DOG DELIGHT 5.25
___ with our Tasty Texas Chili
Serv___ ___ ___rench Fries and Cole Slaw 6.95

CHILI, A Delicious Bowl Full ....

CHI___SIZE
A Bear Pit Burger, Topped with Chili and American
___eese, Served with Our Famous Garlic Toast

TASTER'S TREAT 14.95
Includes Two Pieces Chicken, One Beef Rib, Two
Spareribs, Hefty Portions of Beef and Pork.
Add Cole Slaw, Taters, Bar-B-Q Beans & Garlic Toast

STEAK AND RIBS 14.95
Top Sirloin Steak, Char-Broiled As You Wish, Includes
Baked Beans, Taters, Cole Slaw & Our Great Garlic Toast

HOT LINKS COMBINATIONS
Hot Links & Chicken 9.95
(2 hot links plus 1/4 chicken)
Hot Links & Ribs 12.50
(2 hot links with our famous spareribs)

Treats and Pastries
Chocolate Suicide Cake 3.25
Carrot Cake 3.25
Cheesecake 2.25
Sundaes (Chocolate or Strawberry) 2.95
Hot Fudge Sundae 3.50
Ice Cream (Two Scoops) 2.50

Beverages
Iced Tea 1.75
Coffee, Tea or Decaf 1.25
Milk 1.25/1.75
Chocolate Milk 1.75
Floats 3.50
Thick Malts or Shakes 1.10/1.75
___ 1.10/1.75

LOUISIANA HOT LINKS
Three Spicy Links in Our Special Glaze,
Served with Cole Slaw, BBQ Beans,
French Fries and Garlic Toast
8.95

HUNG___ ___ BEAR
___ DELIGHT
A Whole Side ___
___ B-Q Spareribs
Served with Co___ ___
___B-Q Beans and ___ ___ Fried Taters,
___8.75

BIG B___
"Original" Style D___
and All the Trimmings
(Above Burgers with Cheese X___

GRIZZLY BEAR TREAT
Combination Dinner
Choice of Any Two
of the Following Bar-B-Q Meats:
BEEF, PORK, HAM OR TURKEY
Served with Cole Slaw, Deep Fried Taters,
Bar-B-Q Beans and Garlic Toast
11.95

POLAR BEAR DELIGHT
"Pard, This is Real Eatin'"
A Combination Bar-B-Q Dinner
Consisting of Our Delicious Spareribs
And a Choice of Two:
BEEF, PORK, HAM OR TURKEY
With Cole Slaw, Deep Fried Taters,
Bar-B-Q Beans and Garlic Toast
13.75

Seafood
FRENCH FRIED JUMBO SHRIMP
Served on a Bed of Lettuce with French Fries, C___
Our Own Special Cocktail Sauce and Garlic To___

FISH DINNER
Deep Fried Fish Filets, Served with French F___
___ Slaw and Tartar Sauce

CALLAHAN'S
1213 Wilshire Boulevard, Santa Monica

We were flabbergasted when we first walked into this amazingly unaltered eatery. Its classic, sreamline Moderne clues are about as subtle as a bulldozer in a china shop. Their horizontal neon sign sits over a chrome-covered awning that leads to the curved glass display cases next to the main entrance. A prominent three-striped motif (known as "speedlines") runs throughout the restaurant, including the terrazzo floor. The counter is still covered in the original wood veneer and the formica on the table tops appears to be from when they opened the joint – just unbelievable.

Canetti's Seafood Grotto
309 E. 22nd Street, San Pedro

Established 1949, this was the original City of Los Angeles Immigration Station or the west coast Ellis Island. Joe J. Canetti leases the building from The Port of Los Angeles, which still owns it. Joe's son had since taken over the restaurant and on the day we were there, Joe's grandson stopped in for a late lunch. This is a local treasure few people outside the area are aware of. Our waitress, Liz, told us not to miss the circus at the adjacent Fish Market every Saturday at 4 a.m. That's where the boats dock and Los Angeles's most prestigious restaurants come to buy their fish.

While we talked, DJ entertainer Ron Binkley started to set up his electronic Yamaha with his granddaughter. Ron was still excited from the vintage car cruise they had the night before where he drove Councilwoman Janis Hahn in his 1961 white convertible Impala. He found this beauty in Las Vegas and had paid mucho bucks for it. He checked the levels of his equipment with a bluesy tone reminiscent of Dr. John, then put on a Jerry Lee Lewis CD and worked the growing crowd. We asked him about the Twin Wheel, a western style restaurant/saloon in San Pedro we used to patronize during the 1980s that has since evaporated. As memory serves, aside from the decked out saloon bar that looked like it came out of the gold rush, their claim to fame was their raunchy paintings of topless women covering every one of their walls. Ron remembered it well, his father, a longshoreman, brought him there when he was 10 years old. Sadly, he confirmed that it's indeed gone. He put on Glenn Miller and Patsy Cline and the joint really jumped into gear when Mike Walker, a Caucasian male, put on shades and did his Ray Charles impersonation.

D.J. Ron Binkley on the Yamaha.

Another weekend regular brought an awesome upside down pineapple cake that she shared with everyone. It was still warm. Now a healthy dose of Donna Summers and Ron was on the dance floor with the woman who brought the cake. Liz told us that this was an off day, most of the regulars didn't show. "It's usually like 'Gilligan's Island without the island but with all the coco*nuts*" (stressing nuts), or "it's like the 'Twilight Zone' and you're the star." Food, drink, and fun were off the meter and our total bill was under $5.

Canters

419 N. Fairfax Avenue, Los Angeles

When you enter this converted movie theater, a giant sputnik light embedded in the main column directly ahead beckons you. The deli aroma assaults you. Then, as you walk past the bakery, the low ceiling dramatically opens up, leaving you in the permanent season of…autumn. You are in awe, perplexed, speechless. You cannot resist, you submit to the charm and nostalgia. Looking directly above, the back-lit transcreen of yellow/orange leaves will remind you of a Kodak Colorama ad from the '50s. This is as much

of an East Coast Deli as you can get in Los Angeles The expanded dining room to the north is decorated with a Higgins screen, a terrazzo floor that goes on forever, and giant brass lamps and wall sconces from a romantic era now nearly extinct. This is the time tunnel episode where you fall in love and you don't want to go home.

Canter's long history began in 1924 in Jersey City, New Jersey. In 1931, the Canter brothers move to Boyle Heights, Los Angeles. In 1948, Canter's moved to the Miracle Mile district then took over the Esquire Theater on Fairfax Avenue. Through the years they expanded and opened the Kibbitz Room, where live music can be heard in the lounge/bar. During the 1960s, this was the cool/hip joint to hang out in. Their menu is extensive, with the likes of The Downtowner, Brooklyn Avenue, Eddie Cantor's Delight, Danny Thomas (hot salami on rye), and, of course, the Marilyn (grilled swiss and tomato on rye).

Chili John's

2018 W. Burbank Boulevard, Burbank

In 1913, John Issac licensed the trade name "Chili John" with $40 and opened his restaurant in Green Bay, Wisconsin. Thirty years later he headed west, settled in Burbank, and fed his chili to Lockheed Martin workers around the clock. The story goes that he used to drive back to Wisconsin every year and return with a brand new Cadillac. Now, with the aerospace industry gone, Chili John is still going strong. It sits in a corner brick building with a U-shaped counter and nothing else. Well nothing else except for the giant mural of the Sierra Nevada on the wall.

Their chili is renowned; their unique cooking process requires 400 pounds of high-quality trimmed steak and twenty-four hours. Their business card reads: "Chili John's of California established 1900, famous for being closed." It's true, they are closed for 3 months of the year while they spend the summer in the Sierra Nevada fishing. If you've ever been up there, you wouldn't blame them, you'd most likely join them.

Lake Ediza at the base of the Minarets in the Sierra Nevada, CA.,
imagine fishing here three months of the year.

NOW 8 LOCATIONS

No. 1
3226 Tweedy Blvd.
Lynwood, Calif.
LO. 6-9565

No. 2
Imperial & Paramount
Downey, Calif.
TOpaz 9-9128

No. 3
4141 Long Beach Blvd.
Long Beach at Carson
Long Beach, Calif.
GArfield 7-9227

No. 4
9839 E. Artesia Blvd.
1 Blk. E. of Bellflower Blvd.
Bellflower, Calif.
TOrrey 7-9160

No. 5
11350 E. Washington
Whittier, Calif.
OXford 9-9069

No. 6
9243 Lakewood Blvd.
Downey, Calif.
TOpaz 9-9069

No. 7
9820 Garden Grove Blvd.
Garden Grove, Calif.
LEhi 9-4059

No. 8
13237 Victory Blvd.
Van Nuys, Calif.
Victory at Fulton
POplar 3-9062

CHRIS'& PITT'S
Multiple Locations: Bellflower, Whittier, Downey, & Anaheim

It all started in 1940 when Chris Pelonis opened his dream restaurant with a $2000 loan from his Greek immigrant dad and a prayer. As Chris perfected the recipes for his menu, his popularity grew. Pretty soon, he had eight locations throughout Southern California. Today, the restaurants are still family owned, but they've streamlined down to four locations. The Bellflower store is painted to look like a log cabin from the outside. The neon/flashing bulb sign above the take-out window is a classic 1940s advertising artifact. Counter stools, booths, ceiling fans, even the wide Venetian blinds are all original fixtures. We dined at the Chris' & Pitt's in Van Nuys for almost twenty years before it got flattened...for a Walgreens.

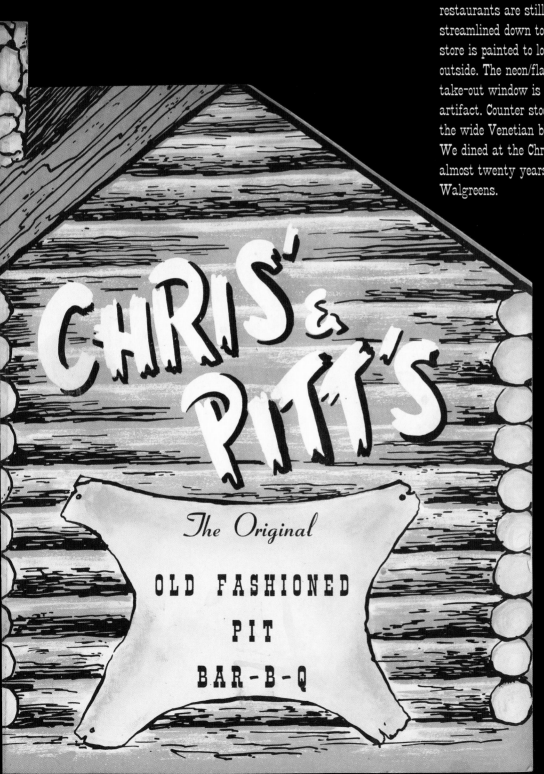

CHRIS' & PITT'S

The Original

OLD FASHIONED

PIT

BAR-B-Q

Clifton's Cafeteria and Bakery
648 S. Broadway, Los Angeles

The story of Clifton's spans over 100 years. It began with David Harrison Clinton in 1888 and continues to this day through five generations of California restaurant owner/operators. Many restaurants of the Clinton's family opened and closed, but the two most famous are Clifton's Pacific Seas and Clifton's Brookdale. After returning from a 1939 Hawaiian vacation, Clifford Clinton and his wife decided to convert their conventional cafeteria on 618 S. Olive Street into a tropical island extravaganza. The front entrance consisted of a multi-layered waterfall, geysers, tropical foliage, and theatrical lighting with a simple sign that read: "Visitors welcome. Pay What You Wish." Inside, this romantic theme was continued with exotic murals, waterfalls, neon palm trees, the Aloha stage, and rain huts that "rained" every twenty minutes. It

98

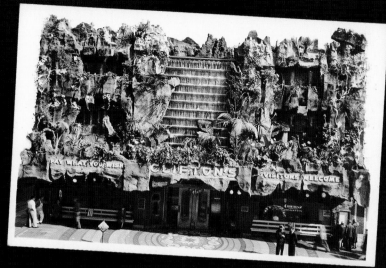

Aloha Clifton's "Pacific Seas"
Olive at Sixth · Los Angeles

Aloha Clifton's "Pacific Seas"
Olive at Sixth · Los Angeles

was so spectacular that it was used in the 1959 movie *Mighty Joe Young* by the same producers that made the original *King Kong*. Sadly, the Pacific Seas closed its doors for good in 1960.

Clifton's Brookdale is still open seven days a week. It opened in 1935 with giant redwoods, a brook, murals, and mechanical animals everywhere. The floor of the front entrance is an Art Deco master-piece featuring L.A. tourist locales, all cast in multi-colored terrazzo. This amazing institution is still family owned and continues their philosophy of humanity and char-ity with their motto: "Pay What You Wish" and "Dine Free Unless Delighted."

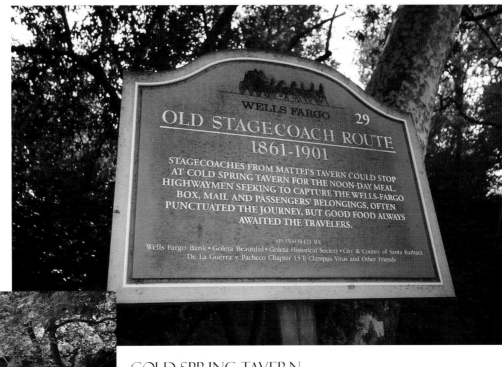

COLD SPRING TAVERN
5995 Stagecoach Road, Santa Barbara

Only fifteen minutes from Santa Barbara yet over 130 years back in time. Originally built in the 1860s as a way station for stagecoach travelers, the Cold Spring Tavern still operates as a first-rate restaurant today. Built by Chinese laborers, this was the very same route General John C. Fremont used in 1848 to capture the city of Santa Barbara.

This place is not some retro wannabe or theme restaurant, it's the real deal, baby. The day we went, the place was so full of bikers that they had motorcycles and people spilling onto the highway itself. They serve Buffalo Burgers, Ribs, Steaks, Lamb, Duck, Rabbit, and Venison (their homemade venison sausages are excellent). If you want a table, you'd better make a reservation ahead of time; make that way, *way* ahead of time.

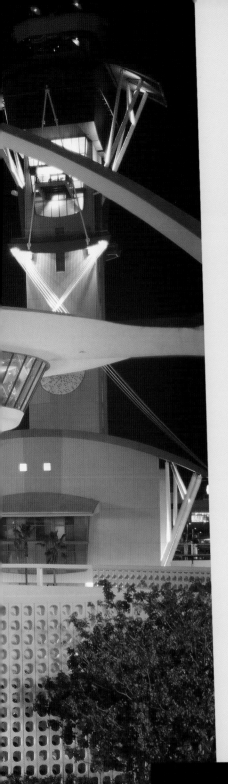

Encounter – LAX Theme Building
209 World Way, L.A. International Airport

This bold, exuberant structure is as impressive today as it was in 1961 when it was completed. It took the combined efforts of three topnotch architectural firms, Pereira and Luckman, Welton Becket and Associates, and Paul R. Williams, to fully realize this extraordinary building.

This Historic-Cultural Monument has often been described as the pinnacle of mid-century Space Age design, a home the Jetsons would have been proud to live in. Two 135-foot high parabolic arches crisscross each other to suspend the circular, saucer-like restaurant 85 feet off the ground. Today it is a Disney-owned restaurant called Encounter. Inspired by the original Star Trek TV series, the interior décor includes amoeba shapes, giant lava lamps, and a drink dispenser/gun that not only looks like, but sounds like, a *phaser* when dispensing booze. Yeah, beam me up, Scotty. Now!

Formosa Café
7156 Santa Monica Boulevard, Hollywood

This classic Hollywood watering hole has a rich movie and gangster history. It started in 1925 when Prizefighter Jimmy Berstein bought a Pacific Electric Red Car and turned it into a lunch car. He partnered with a Chinese cook he knew from Los Angeles's Chinatown. Now the restaurant is owned and operated by his grandson, Vincent Jung. Warner Brothers across the street was the home of the United Artists in an earlier incarnation, and supplied an endless clientele throughout the years. Their walls are covered with over 250 pictures of the movie stars who have dined there since they opened. Not the wannabes that you see in every photo studio all over Hollywood, but the who's who, the crème de la crème, with the likes of Elizabeth Taylor, Marlon Brando, Frank Sinatra, Humphrey Bogart, Grace Kelly, Marilyn Monroe, and Clark Gable. Lana Turner and her gangster boyfriend, Johnny Stompanato, along with his buddies, Mickey Cohen and Bugsy Siegel, were regulars. In fact, Johnny kept his loot in the floor safe of the Star Dining Car. This was where many movie deals were made, aside from being the locations for the movies themselves. Movies like *L.A. Confidential, Swingers,* and *The Majestic.*

The Formosa was slated for demolition in 1991, but lucky for us it was declared an historic landmark and saved.

Golden Pagoda/Hop Louie
950 Mei Ling Way, Chinatown Los Angeles

Opened in 1941, this five-tier pagoda restaurant still serves food vintage of that period. Enter the cocktail lounge on the ground level and listen to the jukebox over exotic drinks. Upstairs on the second level is the main restaurant, which hasn't changed since it opened. Loved by locals, it sits in the heart of Los Angeles's Chinatown. Blogger Lara Jay recalls fondly, "There was a beautiful Chinese woman, in a silk dress, who would play the synth piano in the downstairs bar while we waited for a giant round table complete with lazy susan to be free upstairs. My fav part was her wind-up mechanical monkey that would clack symbols together. The food was greasy and we felt very international."

According to John's father, Albert Eng, Chop Suey was a low-class, low-budget, peasant food that was made from discarded or leftover ingredients. Food for pets, but not quite fit for human consumption. Somehow, white folks took notice, tried it, and liked it. To this day, Albert enjoys telling this story whenever it comes up.

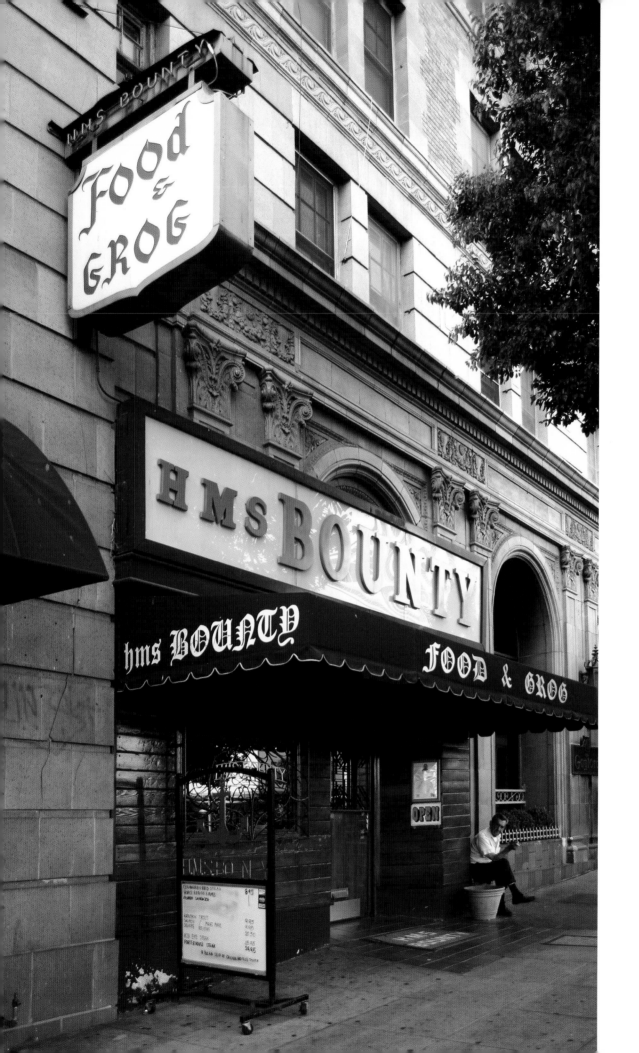

HMS Bounty
3357 Wilshire Boulevard, Los Angeles

Like the Grand Canyon, where you can see the history of our planet through billions of years in one bold slice, Wilshire Boulevard tells the history of Los Angeles along a single street. Wilshire Boulevard starts at Downtown (the heart of the city) and ends at the Pacific Ocean in Santa Monica. MacArthur Park, Chouinard Art Institute, the Ambassador Hotel, the Brown Derby, Perino's. Bullock's Wilshire, the Wiltern, May Co, La Brea Tar Pits, Beverly Hilton Hotel, and the Santa Monica Pier are just the tip of the iceberg along this grand boulevard. Also along this corridor is the Gaylord Hotel/Apartments where the HMS Bounty is located.

Amongst the famous luminaries who dined at the Bounty, Winston Churchill is right up there. He had a meal here while staying at the Ambassador Hotel across the street. There was music, dancing, and tons of booze. Robert Mitchum's sister, Carol, performed here. The Bounty has not changed one iota since the 1940s. It still reeks of old Hollywood glamour (and liquor). It's a prime location for a future Phillip Marlowe film, if there ever was one.

Joe's Café
536 State Street, Santa Barbara

Joe Ferrario opened this eatery in 1928 and things hadn't changed much 'til a recent remodel. This may be the oldest operating restaurant in Santa Barbara. Outside you'll find a terrific neon sign and Spanish tiles. Inside you'll find semi-private booths, copper-plated ceilings, and vintage photographs. This place enjoys excellent reviews for food, booze, and atmosphere.

110

Johnnie's Pastrami
4017 Sepulveda Boulevard, Culver City

A small place with a big reputation. Johnnie's Pastrami is a late-night hangout located off Washington Boulevard in front of another popular stop, Tito's Tacos. Tempting signature pastrami dips, unbeatable crinkle fries and onion rings, all enjoyed in a 1952 diner with tabletop jukeboxes. Or better yet, over a pitcher of beer *al fresco* on the cozy patio warmed by tiki torches and cozy firepits.

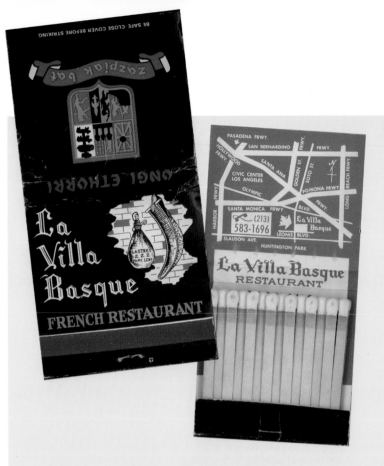

La Villa Basque

2801 Leonis Boulevard, Vernon

La Villa Basque is located in the industrial town of Vernon just south of Downtown Los Angeles. The population of this 5.5 square mile city in 2008 was 80. That's right, 80.

Vernon was founded in 1905 by businessman John Leonis (of Basque origin) and ranchers James J. and Tom Furlon. Initially, it was a cattle town where lawless gunfights were common. According to historian Pete Moruzzi, "…Entrepreneur Jack Doyle opened what was billed as 'the longest bar in the world' in 1907. It had thirty-seven bartenders, thirty-seven cash registers, and a sign advising 'if your children need shoes, don't buy booze."

During the 1920s and 1930s Vernon was home to U.S. and Bethlehem Steel, Alcoa Aluminum, Owens Glass, Studebaker, and numerous other factories aside from the iconic Farmer John's Meat Packing Plant. The mural surrounding the entire Farmer John's compound was originally painted by Leslie A. Grimes, who fell to his death from a scaffold while painting this mural. Founding father John Leonis' grandson, Leonis Malburg, has been on city council since the mid-1950s. In 1974, he became the mayor and still runs the city today. No talk of term limits here.

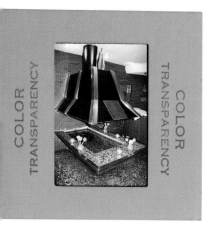

Leon's Steak House
10945 Victory Boulevard,
North Hollywood

Back in 1945, Leon's was a popular outpost for nearby Lockheed Martin employees who would grab a lunch in the coffee shop, or stop in after their shift for cocktails and prime rib in the steak house. Big Band headliners and karaoke remained in full swing all the way up to closing when piano bar legend Buddy Worth and the Bill Davies Orchestra played for the last time to a SRO house. Originally owned by

Leon Grown, Leon's remained a family owned business until 1992 when chef Marco Medina and bartender Javier Morelos took ownership. Years ago, they started out as dishwashers who could barely speak English. Leon's Steak House was demolished for a CVS Pharmacy in 2003.

Photo by Adrienne Biondo

115

MADONNA INN

Madonna Inn
100 Madonna Road, San Luis Obispo

Alex and Phyllis Madonna's roadside masterpiece is legendary in California. Most people traveling Highway 101 between Los Angeles and San Francisco will have stopped here and experienced the flamboyant decor that would've made Liberace blush. This is a one-stop everything, complete with hotel, motel, restaurants, pool, spa, shops, and, at one time, even a gas station. Each of their 109 rooms boasts a unique and individual concept. Rooms like: Barrel of Fun, Bit of Solvang, Caveman Room, Cloud Nine, Hideaway, Jungle Rock, Love Nest, Pony Room, Safari, Swiss Belle, Time of Your Life, Wilhelm Tell, and Yahoo. The Madonna Inn also features banquet rooms, a bakery, Copper Café, Steak House, and Silver Bar with dancing and live entertainment. In 2005, they opened a 20,000 sq. ft. Expo Center.

117

Closing day at the Matterhorn Chef. Chef/owner Unebule at far right, Tony Hortenstein on accordion, Unebule's wife and co-owner at far left, 2006.

Matterhorn Chef/
Old Heidelberg (now Barone's)

13726 Oxnard Street, Van Nuys

Established in 1958, Old Heidelberg was a San Fernando Valley favorite, serving fine German cuisine. You had to walk through a giant wine barrel before entering the lobby. In the 1980s it became the popular Matterhorn Chef, serving authentic schnitzel, sauerbraten, and rouladen hasenpfeffer. Customers sang and danced to German tunes, not to mention songs from "The Sound of Music." Chef/owner Unebule and his wife sang and performed along with other entertainers like accordionist Tony Hortenstein, musician extraordinaire. Believe it or not, Tony came from Austria to perform in the 1939 New York World's Fair and, lucky for us, he never left. The Matterhorn Chef closed in 2006.

118

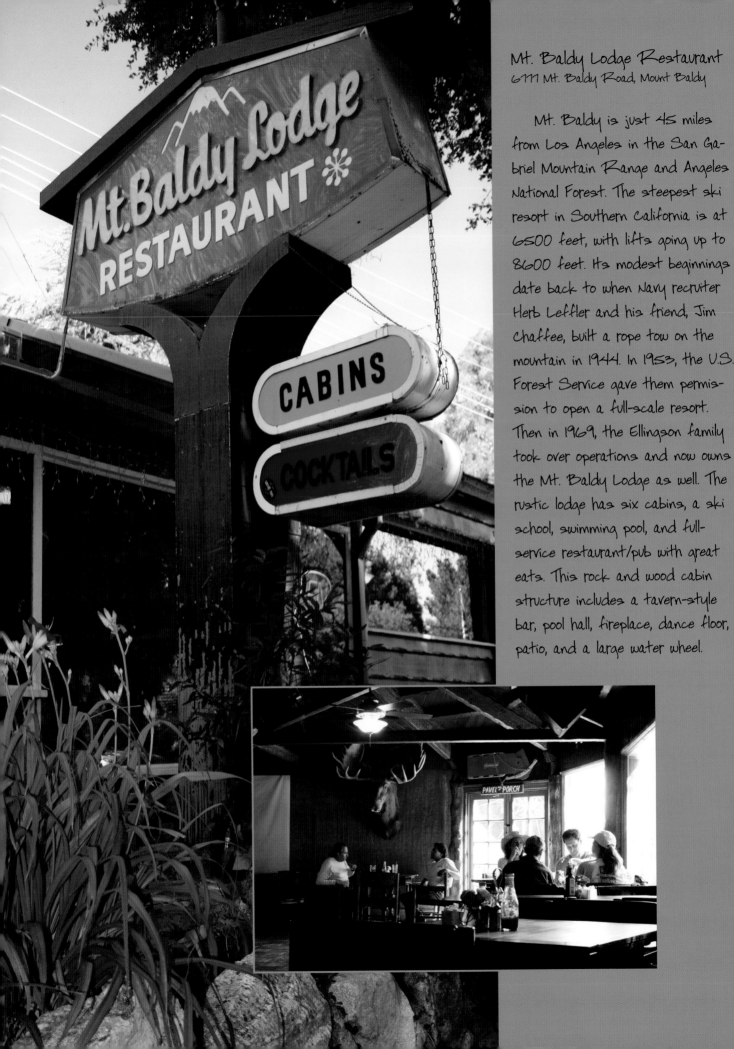

Mt. Baldy Lodge Restaurant
6777 Mt. Baldy Road, Mount Baldy

Mt. Baldy is just 45 miles from Los Angeles in the San Gabriel Mountain Range and Angeles National Forest. The steepest ski resort in Southern California is at 6500 feet, with lifts going up to 8600 feet. Its modest beginnings date back to when Navy recruiter Herb Leffler and his friend, Jim Chaffee, built a rope tow on the mountain in 1944. In 1953, the U.S. Forest Service gave them permission to open a full-scale resort. Then in 1969, the Ellingson family took over operations and now owns the Mt. Baldy Lodge as well. The rustic lodge has six cabins, a ski school, swimming pool, and full-service restaurant/pub with great eats. This rock and wood cabin structure includes a tavern-style bar, pool hall, fireplace, dance floor, patio, and a large water wheel.

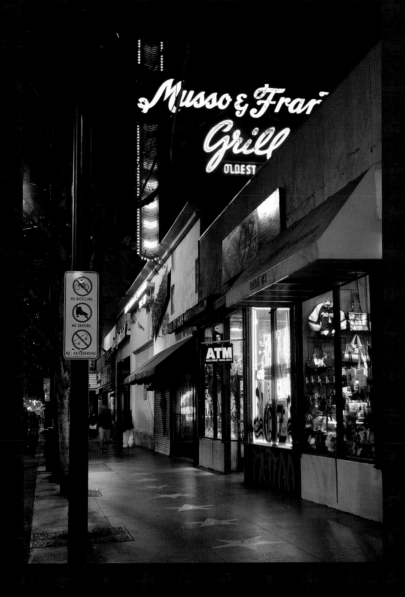

Musso & Frank Grill
6667 Hollywood Boulevard, Hollywood

This true Hollywood icon could be the most authentic, unmolested classic old style restaurant left in Los Angeles. Originally from Oregon, Joseph Musso came to Los Angeles and partnered with Frank Toulet for their culinary venture Musso & Frank Grill in 1919. They sold the restaurant to Joseph Carissimi and John Mosso in 1926. Apparently the back room was the 'hang out' for the creative types including writers. Hacks like F. Scott Fitzgerald, William Faulkner, Raymond Chandler, Erskine Caldwell, Lillian Hellman, Thomas Wolfe, Dorothy Parker, and Dashiell Hammett were regulars. Other regulars included Charlie Chaplin, Ernest Hemingway, composer Igor Stravinsky, and Charles Bukowski. The last time we were there, we spotted Ron Jeremy (yes, he had one girl on each arm).

The food is excellent, with a new menu everyday. How do we know? The date is printed on the top. The atmosphere here is so thick, it's like diving into a pool of Jell-O®. From the furniture to the fixtures to the murals on the walls, hardly anything has changed in nearly a hundred years. Time capsule? You bet.

The 94th Aero Squadron
Raymer Avenue, Van Nuys

The 94th Aero Squadron is inviting from the minute you approach and are greeted by a military jeep with its headlights on and a bombed-out World War I building. Enjoy French country-style dining by candlelight with piped-in Muzak and 1960s film themes. There's also a hopping upstairs/downstairs cocktail lounge. Squadron walls are covered with photos of nearby Lockheed Aircraft and Rosie the Riveter wartime workers, with authentic aircraft gauges, artifacts, and artillery combining to recreate a world that recalls America at its most patriotic. There's even a specially reserved "pilots only" table. Many a summer evening is spent here watching the planes land at Van Nuys Airport and enjoying a cocktail by the fire pits.

North Woods Inn

North Woods Inn/Clearman's Restaurants
Multiple Locations: San Gabriel, Covina & La Mirada

Thanks to founder John Clearman, we can experience the rustic charm of a log cabin themed restaurant from yesteryear at the North Woods Inn. It's easy to picture yourself in the Yukon mining for gold as you approach these massive, snow-covered structures. The snow on these roofs never melts though. At the La Mirada location, you are welcomed by a giant Polar Bear. Not only can you eat peanuts at all the locations, but you can even toss the shells right onto the sawdust floors. Tiffany-style lamps barely illuminate the vast cocktail lounge/bar. The menu features steak and seafood, with cheese bread dripping with butter. Don't come here if you want to lose weight.

The San Gabriel location opened in 1966, with a little hamburger stand called Clearman's Galley installed two years later. The Galley, affectionately known as "The Boat," was a real 1913 boat that originally performed mail service duty between San Francisco and Alaska. A popular after-work hangout and sports bar, The Boat was always busy; that is, until Kohl's decided to build a store on-site. Despite community protests, The Boat was dismantled and later reported to have "fallen apart" while it was being moved. R.I.P.

1001 N. Alameda Street, Los Angeles

Opened October, 1908, this quintessential Angeleno Noir eatery is legendary. They just celebrated their 100-year anniversary. Philippe's has a seating capacity of 350, seventy-five employees, two parking lots, and also happens to be right across the street from Union Station. This place still has sawdust on the floor, 1940s style telephone booths, an old school candy counter, communal tables, a train museum, and for the longest time, coffee for the depression price of nine cents (it's now a quarter). They're known for their famous French dipped sandwiches and their mustard is the "bomb." Apparently French immigrant Philipe Matieu accidentally dropped a sandwich in meat juices one day and the rest is history. Remember, cash only here.

SAM'S SEAFOOD

Sam's Seafood/Kona Restaurant
16278 Pacific Coast Highway, Huntington Beach

New owners, new menu, but the same Pacific Island theme. A wonderfully expanded menu has something for everyone. Island buffet, tiki bar, Thursday karaoke, happy hour, custom tiki carving by Chuck Stone, exotic music and dance from the South Pacific. This place is certainly one of the top five Tiki joints in the state. Dine in a 1960s South Seas paradise, complete with waterfalls and vintage murals of the Islands! If only they could bring back the pay phones mounted inside giant clam shells. It is self-described as "A Polynesian Spectacular," and who are we to disagree? Kona is just a few steps away from the Harbor House, Woody's Diner, and the unique water tower that's been converted to a residence but always seems to be on the market.

Tony's on the Pier
210 Fisherman's Wharf, Redondo Beach

Also known as Old Tony's, this has been a South Bay destination since 1958, sitting atop the Redondo Beach pier like a chopped off lighthouse. You can't get much more romantic than sipping Old Tony's delicious Mai Tai's around the circa 1960s circular firepit, or heading up to their second-floor lounge, known as the Top of Tony's. Afterwards, enjoy a cozy dinner with a golden Pacific sunset as your backdrop. If that's not enough, you get Tony's famous souvenir glass with each Mai Tai you order. They've got live music Wednesday through Sunday nights, food, a cool sea breeze, and did we mention drinks? It's the most fun you can have without getting arrested. Go, for cryin' out loud.

The Trails
Route 66-Huntington Drive, Duarte

This was a true Route 66 ranch-style supper club, built in 1951. Steaks at The Trails were terrific, and there was nothing like watching the seniors arriving dressed to the nines to strut their Big-Band stuff. Singer after singer would belt out classic numbers like "Fly Me to the Moon" in the Trails' lounge. Organist Jim McEwan was accompanied on percussion by diners who kept time by shaking Pringles potato chip cylinders filled with rice and covered in gift wrap. By 2002, rumors of a condo development surfaced and the restaurant closed suddenly, without notice. Employees arrived to find the door padlocked. Even Jim was locked out, along with his organ. Today, little is left to tell the story of The Trails. Even the dedication plaque was stolen by recycling vandals in 2008.

29 Palms Inn Restaurant
73950 Inn Avenue, 29 Palms

This is a one of the best kept secrets in all of Southern California, known mostly to locals and the few tight lipped L.A. weekenders hip to this region. You can't beat the food (fresh vegetables from their own garden) or relaxed desert atmosphere. In the Palms at the Oasis of Mara since 1928, this jewel in the desert is next to the entrance of one of the most whimsical, magical places in California, Joshua Tree National Park. They are also near the mysterious "Integratron" and Pioneertown. Without fail, we always feel a tinge of sadness when we exit their gate and see their stop sign, which reads: "It's your choice."

Villa Terraza Restaurant
9955 Sunland Boulevard, Shadow Hills

Formally the Old Vienna, this mini village is somewhat hidden in the horse ranches of Shadow Hills. Some sections of the main restaurant along with the corner tower were built from river rocks found on site. The back banquet room was rumored to have hosted the likes of Frank Sinatra (something we hear often). There is also a tunnel to the north side of the property up against the hill they call "The Cave." George, the owner, believes that this was originally the wine cellar, maybe. While growing up in nearby Tujunga, Adriene recalled stories of World War II Nazi war criminals hiding out in this place. Co-incidence? Perhaps...

Vince's Spaghetti
Multiple Locations: Ontario, Rancho Cucamonga, Torrance, & Temecula

Vince's would win any popularity contest, hands down. In 1945, Grandma Rose, Vincent Cuccia, and his two brothers opened the original Vince's restaurant in Ontario, CA, a six-stool food stand in the middle of orange groves. The original menu was comprised of orange juice, fresh fruit, and French Dip Sandwiches. Grandma Rose would prepare the food in the kitchen then walk it to the customers some fifty yards away. Unable to recreate the food they were used to in their native Chicago, they created their own recipe for spaghetti and sauce, which are still used today. In the early 1970s, Vince sold his share and moved his family to Torrance to open their own restaurant while his two brothers continued operating the Vince's in Ontario and Rancho Cucamonga. Families travel for many miles to experience the charm of this Chicago-style Italian restaurant that is still going strong.

The Warehouse Restaurant
4499 Admiralty Way, Marina Del Rey

Experience the tropics in Marina Del Rey. Created in 1969 by international photographer Burt Hixson in a pre-Indiana Jones safari/Amazon/ nautical/exotic setting, this two-story restaurant offers magnificent views of the marina, and should you time it right, spectacular sunsets. The moat at the restaurant entrance is teeming with hefty koi fish, while the inside reveals an iron cage elevator in its world famous "crate and barrel" dining rooms. The lobby has just as many celebrity photos as the Formosa Cafe. Stars like Robert Stack, Lloyd Bridges, Ernest Borgnine, Rodney Dangerfield, Connie Stevens, and Ann Miller, all taken in the 1970s. Live entertainment, happy hour, steak, ribs, and seafood (try the Coconut Mahi Mahi) are served by candlelight, inside or out.

Wheel Inn Restaurant
50900 Seminole Drive, Cabazon

The Wheel Inn is right next to the giant dinosaurs built by Claude Bell back in 1960s and made famous in *Pee Wee's Big Adventure*. Rumor has it that Claude had visited Lucy the Elephant in Margate, New Jersey, as a child. He was so impressed that years later, he was compelled to build his own masterpiece. Claude ran the pastel-portrait studio in Knott's Berry Farm and, like Simon Rodia who built the landmark Watts Towers on his own free time, constructed these dinosaurs in concrete and steel. Eleven short years and a quarter of a million dollars poorer, he had a 150-foot-long Brontosaurus (later renamed Apatosaurus) nicknamed Dinny. The stairway from the tail entrance leads up to the gift shop located in the belly. A single dinosaur is a lonely sight to behold so, in 1981, a sixty-five-foot Tyrannosaurus named Rex was created to accompany the giant lizard. Orange County developer Gary Kanter bought the property in 2005 and is now preaching intelligent design from these twin dinosaurs.

Cabazon is a typical truck stop turned tourist attraction in the middle of the desert just off I-10. The restaurant is open 24-7 and the waitresses dress like Pebble Flintstone. Don't forget, the velvet paintings on the walls are for sale. Buy one of Elvis before it becomes unaffordable.